Mermaid Mess

Written by Lisa Thompson
Pictures by Craig Smith and Lew Keilar

"Mermaid ahead!" said Bones, the sea dog, from the lookout.

"Shiver me topsails!" said Captain Red Beard. He grabbed his telescope. "The mermaid is inviting us over."

Captain Red Beard knew it was bad luck to say no to a mermaid.

"Thank you for stopping," said the mermaid. "I'm moving into a new cave, but my mermaid treasure box is stuck in the rocks. Would you help me to get it out?"

"Did you say treasure?" asked Lizzie, the first mate.

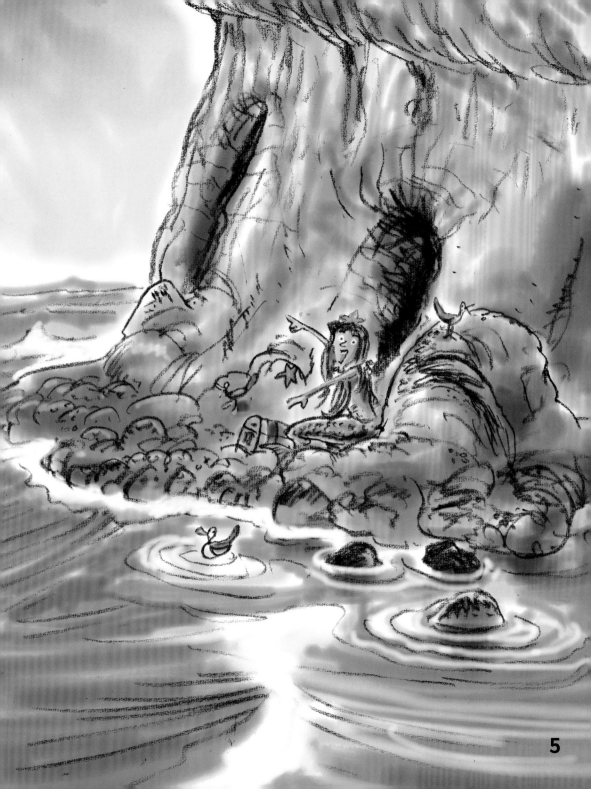

Captain Red Beard knew it was bad luck to say no to a mermaid.

"Dirty rotten pirates," said Fingers, the parrot.

Captain Red Beard asked the mermaid to tie a rope around her treasure box. The crew grabbed the other end of the rope.

"Heave-ho," said Captain Red Beard. The crew pulled and pulled.

The treasure box squeaked and moaned but it did not budge. It was still stuck in the rocks.

The Captain joined the crew at the end of the rope. "Heave-ho!" said the Captain again.

The mermaid's treasure box flew out from between the rocks. The treasure box hit another rock and burst open. Hundreds of pieces of seaweed scattered everywhere.

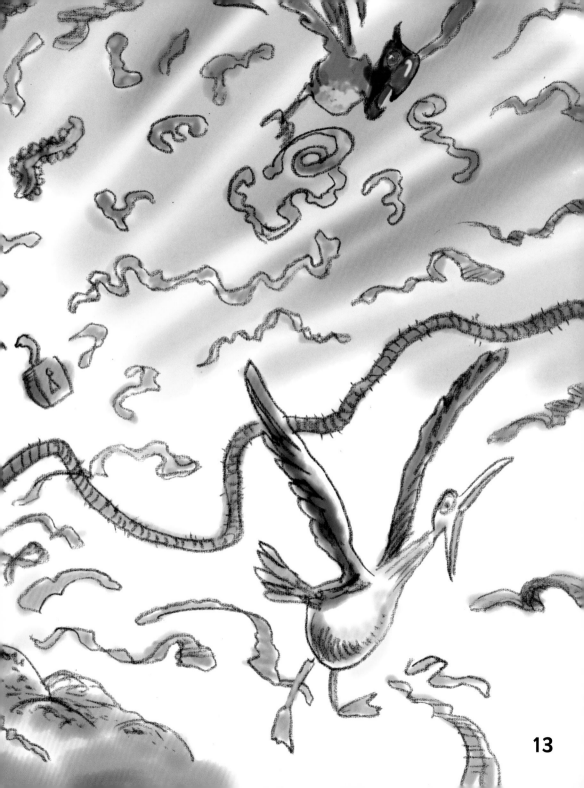

13

"What a mess," said Bones, the sea dog.

The mermaid was unhappy. "My seaweed treasure!" she cried.

"Seaweed treasure?" said Captain Red Beard. He wanted to laugh.

"You must help me collect it all," said the mermaid.

The Captain knew it was bad luck to say no to a mermaid.

"Lower the boat. We must help the mermaid collect the seaweed," said the Captain.

They collected every last bit of seaweed treasure.

"Thank you so much," said the mermaid. "I don't know what I would do without my treasure. Could you do one more thing for me before you leave?"

"Yes," said the Captain.

"My new cave is full of junk. Could you take it with you?" she asked.

The Captain knew it was bad luck to say no to a mermaid.

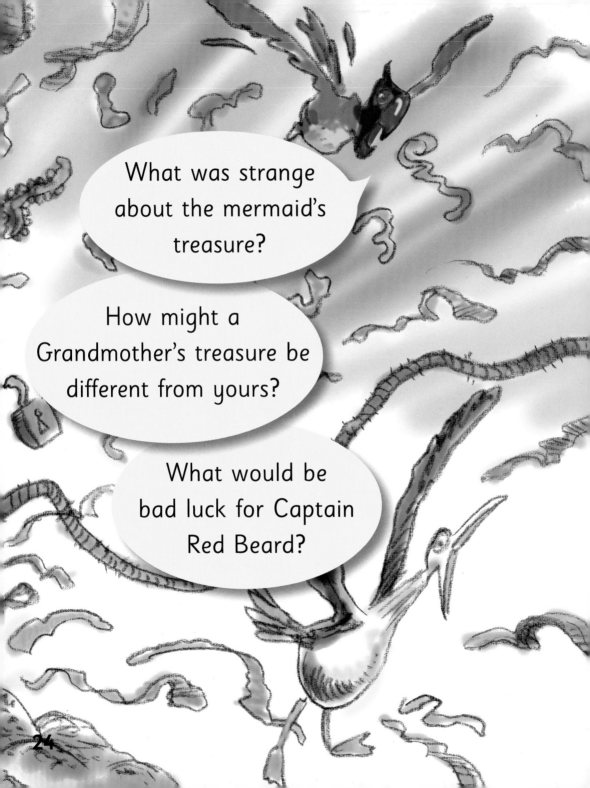

What was strange about the mermaid's treasure?

How might a Grandmother's treasure be different from yours?

What would be bad luck for Captain Red Beard?

24